I first met Mary when she and her husband came to our church in Northwest Melbourne about eight years ago. From the moment I met her I was drawn to her joyful and enthusiastic faith in Jesus. Mary has a passion for wanting people set free from spiritual bondages and past hurts. She has sought the Lord with diligence to learn biblical strategies to guide people to freedom through repentance and prayer. Her faith in the supernatural power of the Holy Spirit's work in our lives has driven her to continually encourage the people she meets not to settle for anything less than the freedom Jesus promised in His word.

This book is a powerful summary of the tried and tested techniques, and strategies Mary has learnt as she has ministered to hundreds of people over her ministry. What a blessing to those of us who also minister to others to now have this priceless resource from a champion in the kingdom!

MELISSA MAHER
Senior Pastor INChurch Melbourne

Birthed from decades of experience in Christian Biblical counseling, countless life changing moments of people connecting with their freedom in Christ, and years of prayer, teaching and instilling God's word into others, Mary has poured herself into this 'manual' towards freedom, not as a tool for the counselor only but to any reader!

It contains her most valued practical resources, scriptures and guidance on the steps to true freedom in Jesus Christ! We have used every single one of these resources in counselling within our church, have equipped many Pastors and leaders with these to empower them to walk with people through trials.

I truly believe this incredible step of obedience to share it with as many people as possible, is going to enrich and empower individuals and organisations globally!

Mary is truly an example of what it means to wholeheartedly know and experience the Holy Spirit and the true freedom that He brings.

HANNAH VAN ROOYEN<br>
Senior Pastor CRC Gaborone Botswana

# WHAT MOST SHRiNKS
*Can't Tell You*

A practical guide to setting the captives free

## MARY JALALABADI

Published by Mary Jalalabadi
maryjalalabadi1951@gmail.com

First published 2009
2nd Edition 2025, Updated

Copyright © Mary Jalalabadi, 2025

The moral right of the author has been asserted.

All rights reserved. Without limiting the rights under copyright restricted above, no part of this publication may be reproduced, stored in or introduced into a retrieval system, or transmitted, in any form or by any means (electronic, mechanical, photocopying, recording or otherwise), without the prior written permission of the copyright owner and publisher of this book.

Scripture taken from the New International Version
Copyright © 1973, 1978, 1984
International Bible Society
Used by permission of Zondervan Bible Publishers.

Scripture taken from the New King James Version
Copyright © 1982 by Thomas Nelson Inc
Used by permission. All rights reserved.

Scripture taken from the Amplified Bible
Copyright © 1954, 1958, 1962, 1964, 1987
Used by permission of the Lockman Foundation
and the Zondervan Corporation.

Diagram from Masterlife Discipleship Training for Leaders
Copyright © 1980, 1982 The Sunday School Board of the
Southern Baptist Convention. All rights reserved.
Revised 1982, Reprinted 1983. Used with Permission.

 A catalogue record for this book is available from the National Library of Australia

ISBN: 978 1 7643042 0 7 (pbk)
ISBN: 978 1 7643042 1 4 (ebk)

Cover designed by Hannah van Rooyen
Cover illustration by Amy Walters/Dreamstime.com
Author photo by Ramon Tranquim
Typeset by Blue Wren Books
Printed by Ingram Spark

# Foreword

Seldom in life do we come across people whose authenticity and humility touch you deeply. Mary Jalalabadi and her husband Ashok are two of those people.

I remember first meeting them at our church many years ago when we first started attending. We had learnt about this dynamic, supposedly retired missionary pastors who had come out of retirement and were teaching the Church's Bible College. I attended some of those courses and was always inspired by the power, authority and clarity with which they conferred the word. Theirs is not a faith based on hearsay. Theirs is a faith that has been etched out of many years working and toiling in the Lord's harvest fields.

As my relationship with them grew, they became mentors, and I came to realise that these were not mere mortals. These were stalwarts in the faith, and the lessons that I've learnt from them have helped me navigate some of life's big challenges. Some of those lessons have been etched in the words of this book.

I remember wanting to help some Christian friends who were experiencing some emotional and personal challenges but for whom I realised that "the conventional" provided stark limitations. They were dealing with past hurts and perceived injustices that had corroded relationships and threatened their faith, and I knew that there was a spiritual dimension that had to be addressed. Enter Mary.

She shared with me the principles written within this book that are purposed to help others attain the victory that they have in Christ. These principles are not mere theoretical knowledge. As a mental health doctor, I have first-hand seen and used the works and theories that have helped people come out of their mental and emotional challenges. This is different. This incorporates the spiritual element, something that can so often be overlooked. These principles are as timeless as they are powerful, as they should be, given that they stem from scripture.

This is not a book to be read as a mere academic exercise or to titillate your impulses. Read this book if you want to be equipped to help other believers attain the freedom that they have in Christ. This is a manual for the fervent Christian who wants to see others attain that freedom and start walking in victory.

DR PASCHAL ALEXANDER
Mental Health Practitioner

# Contents

| | | |
|---|---|---|
| *Acknowledgements* | | ix |
| *A note from the Author* | | xi |
| | Introduction | 1 |
| 1. | Basic Overview | 5 |
| 2. | How to Begin | 11 |
| 3. | Contributing Factors to Emotional or Mental Struggles | 15 |
| 4. | How to Encourage them to Share | 19 |
| 5. | Genogram | 25 |
| 6. | Do they have any idea of the War Zone they are in? | 31 |
| 7. | How to Work Through Their Genogram | 37 |
| 8. | Dealing with the Zigzags | 43 |
| 9. | Possible Blockages in their Belief System | 47 |
| 10. | Different Areas of Need | 53 |
| 11. | A Few Examples | 63 |
| 12. | What about Deliverance Ministry? | 69 |

# Acknowledgements

I would like to express my grateful thanks to my husband, Ashok, who is my life partner and friend of adventure. You have been my faithful helper, observer/chaperone over the years and especially when I have ministered to men. You've been on the other end of the phone when I couldn't find the Scripture reference I needed, you've given suggestions for re-wording different sentences, have proofread it, and when I've felt like chucking it all in you've encouraged me to persevere. I love you very much.

To my three children, Nalini, Samuel and Hannah, I love you all very much. You have witnessed the change in countless people who have received freedom in Christ as I have shared various aspects of this book with them, and you are already using some of these diagrams to show other people the way to freedom in Christ. All three of you have encouraged me to get this down as a legacy and to pass it on. So, here is the baton, now you can run with it!

# A note from the Author

Having spent over 20 years in Africa, some of the material included here has been gleaned from fellow Christians and notes handed out at meetings, etc. If any of the material requires copyright permission, please contact me so that I can obtain the necessary permission for future editions.

# Introduction

Whereas secular doctors, psychologists and psychiatrists are playing a vital role in helping people remain fit and healthy physically, emotionally, and mentally, unless they are born-again Christians they will not have the necessary resources to help their clients overcome spiritual issues. They are certainly able to help assist them by showing them how to control their depression, anger, fear, and unforgiveness, etc., but are unable to show them how to be set free from them.

As Dr Neil T. Anderson says, "Secular research assumes that we are an evolutionary product of our past environment and shaped by our individual choices. Such research makes no attempt to show the potential of a new life in Christ or what a Spirit-filled life could be."[1]

All people have been created in the image of God (Genesis 1:27), which means we are tripartite beings that are made up of spirit, soul, and body. Therefore, whatever affects one of these areas affects the whole person.

For years now, as part of Christian ministry, I have spent time praying with and for people who have been struggling to enjoy life. In most cases, after enquiring a bit deeper it has become clear that pain from the past has not been dealt with and this has been a key trigger to their depression, attempted suicide, self-harm, anger, and a whole host of other responses. Many have

---

1  Dr Neil T. Anderson, Bondage Breaker

tried coping with it or burying their pain with alcohol, drugs, busyness, or pornography, etc., but have not known how to deal with it.

Jesus came to set the captives free, and yet there are still so many people who are in torment of soul because of past pain inflicted by others or by themselves, or from having a poor self-image. Because they are made up of spirit, soul, and body, this means each area needs to be cared for. Oftentimes, medication is required to help balance emotions and their body chemistry but as progress is made in these areas, the client is often deemed 'better'. Once the symptoms are alleviated, the person carries on with life 'normally' and yet a seemingly simple situation may trigger a totally unexpected response. In this regard, it is rather like putting a plaster over a festering sore. The root cause of the problem must be dealt with first and then healing will come.

As we prayerfully seek the Lord's face, the Holy Spirit will reveal the Word that brings forth healing. Then, with teaching and an understanding of basic spiritual laws, they are able to co-operate with and actively seek the freedom and healing that Christ died to give them.

From the time I was born-again I could see beyond people's smiles to some of the struggles they were facing. I didn't necessarily know what their struggles were, but I knew they were struggling. As I greeted them, some responded openly when I asked, "Are you **really** fine?" but others avoided me because they knew I could see beyond their smiling veneer. As time went on, people started coming for 'a chat' because they needed to get something off their chest. As they began trusting me with their confidences, word slowly started going around and more and more people came for a time of prayer and sharing. I had wrongly presumed that ALL Christians could see what I saw but it was only years later that I realised that this was a gift from the Lord.

The methods I use have been developed over years of practical 'hands-on' experience. As I gain more insight from the Word of God and from other godly counsellors, I adapt my methods accordingly. I trust that what is presented here will help give some practical "how-to's" on showing people who are spiritually bound, the way to freedom in Christ.

*Chapter 1*
## Basic Overview

It is essential to understand the power of prayer and the importance of being in an attitude of prayer before meeting with someone to show them the way to freedom in Christ. The Holy Spirit is the One who will guide you into all truth, and at the end of the day, it's the truth of God's Word that sets people free and not any of your own clever ideas. The more memory verses you are familiar with, the better. Have a good working knowledge of the Word of God and develop your own bank of Scriptures that you can refer to quickly. Make sure you have a good concordance or mobile phone available, so when the Holy Spirit brings a verse or passage to mind you can look it up quickly. A Google search using some of the key words in the verse will highlight the exact or similar Scriptures very quickly.

The Scriptures I frequently use are:

Genesis 1:26–27; Genesis 3:1–13; Psalm 119:130; Proverbs 28:13 (NIV); Isaiah 61:1–3; Jeremiah 29:11; Jonah 1:1–15; Matthew 3:10; Matthew 6:14–15; Matthew 18:19–20; Matthew 18:21–35; Matthew 28:18–20; John 5:1–9; John 8:31–32; John 10:10; John 15:1–17; Romans 12:1–2; 2Corinthians 10:3–5; Ephesians 6:10–18; Colossians 2:9–10; Colossians 2:13–15; 2 Timothy 1:7; Hebrews 11:1 (AMP); Hebrews 12:15; James 4:7–8; 1 John 1:9; 1 John 5:14–15.

Some Key Steps:

**1. Show you care**

If your primary motivation in spending time praying for people is to pick up the latest gossip, leave now! This ministry is for those who have a heart for the hurting, have a desire to see the captives set free, and for folks to enjoy the abundant life that Christ promised.

Always have someone nearby in case a challenging situation presents itself, the person is unknown to you, or if you feel there may be some demonic oppression present. Only see people from the opposite sex if they are willing to see you with an observer from their same gender present.

**2. Choose the venue carefully**

Your Pastor is God's chosen shepherd for the flock, and he has to protect them from even well-meaning Christians, so it's good to share with him the kind of ministry that God has placed on your heart. Some people may feel somewhat intimidated if you arrange to see them in a church office, in which case, try and choose a neutral venue for the initial contact: a coffee bar, garden or beach etc. If the church is the best place for you to see people, make sure they are comfortable with meeting you there and that someone is present in the background at the church office. It's important to have people in the background in order to protect yourself, the person you are seeing, and your church, in case of any misunderstanding. I have seen the Lord meet with people and set them free in a great variety of places, including coffee shops!

After welcoming them, offer them a cup of tea or coffee to help them relax a bit and have a glass of water and a box of tissues handy too. Minimise distractions by making sure phones are turned off or muted, pets are out of sight and hearing, children are suitably occupied, and background noise is eliminated as far as possible.

### 3. Encourage them to bring their own Bible

Whether you are or whether you are not a trained counsellor, make it absolutely clear that you will be sharing principles from the Word of God, because this is your reference book. With all the political correctness flying around these days, it is important NOT to call yourself a counsellor unless of course you are a trained one! Invite them for Care and Prayer or Share and Prayer or whatever you or your Pastor want to call it.

Make sure they have a sound version of the Bible, as there are some versions out there that deny that Jesus Christ is THE one and only Son of God, e.g. The New World Translation. Encourage them to bring a translation of the Bible that they use regularly or is easily understood, e.g. the NIV, NKJV, Amplified, etc.

When you share Scriptures with them from the Word of God, encourage **them** to read the passage aloud from their own Bible. This is really important because what I find is, that as **they** read the passage of Scripture it brings revelation to them. Also, in reading aloud, a proclamation is being made into the heavenly realms. Do not forget, you are engaging in spiritual warfare when you meet with people to show them the way to freedom in Christ.

*The thief does not come except to steal, and to kill, and to destroy. I have come that they may have life, and that they may have it more abundantly.*

JOHN 10:10 NKJV

Some have refused point blank to read aloud, which might mean they are not too confident with themselves, their reading skills, or God, but it can also indicate a measure of wanting to be in control. The worst-case scenario could indicate that there is some demonic influence present. Make a mental note of this, but whatever the reason is, as long as they are happy for you to continue, read the passage aloud so that the truth is proclaimed.

## 4. Simple Codes of Conduct

Psychologically, they need to have an escape route, so don't block the door! Try and sit opposite them, in comfortable chairs which are slightly at an angle to each other. This gives them opportunity to look straight ahead without having you staring back at them. Sit at the same level as them because they will feel intimidated if you are seated higher than they are. If you are seated lower than them your authority can seem diminished to both you and them. Definitely do not sit too close to them as they may feel somewhat uncomfortable or threatened!

Reassure them that whatever is shared between the two of you will remain strictly confidential, unless there are situations that have legal or serious medical implications. Tell them you may need to make some notes to help keep you on track. Let them know that any Scriptures or diagrams used during the session will be handed over to them at the end of your time together.

Try to keep your arms and hands relaxed on your lap or resting on the arms of your chair and lean slightly forward to show interest in what they are saying. Don't lean back with arms folded or crossed over your head, legs crossed, or reclining back in the chair, as these show either closed or aggressive body language or even too casual an approach, which can be off-putting.

Make good eye contact with them but do not stare them out! Staring out of the window, flicking your pen, checking your watch, or flipping through papers will give them the impression that you are not really interested in what they have to say, and rightly so.

## 5. Avoid too much physical Contact

A handshake in greeting is often more than sufficient, unless you know the person quite well, in which case, a short hug is also appropriate. When working with them try to avoid too much physical contact, as mixed signals can be received. If there are tears of emotion, perhaps a touch of reassurance on the arm or shoulder, handing them a tissue, or praying a quick prayer for strength for them would be appropriate. A hug may be in order but do not linger over the hug. You may have to work at relaxing initially but the more you relax the more they will relax too.

If they are comfortable with reading the Bible aloud in my presence, I will often ask them to read from their own translation of the Bible the Scriptures that the Holy Spirit quickens to my heart. As they read the passage aloud, I have found that it often results in them receiving revelation from the Lord.

*The entrance of Your words gives light;*
*It gives understanding to the simple.*
                    PSALM 119:130 NKJV

*Chapter 2*
## How to Begin

After having greeted the person who has come for Care and Prayer, offer them a cool drink, a cup of tea or coffee, and share some small talk with them to help them relax.

If they are people I have not seen before, I generally ask them to share how they came into a personal relationship with our Lord Jesus Christ.

It's good to ask them what they would like to see happen as you share together, then start your time together by opening in prayer. Occasionally, after having seen them before, I will ask them to open in prayer. If they feel uncomfortable about doing so, then I will open in prayer.

Some people come wanting a 'Quick Fix' or a 'Magic Wand' waved over them so that all their problems will fade away in an instant. Their reasoning is that you as the pastor or church leader have a special 'in' with 'The Man Upstairs.' In such cases, I remind them that I can show them the way to freedom in Christ, but I cannot do it for them. As they appropriate the truth of God's Word by faith, they will be set free.

Whereas I have seen countless people receive almost instant freedom as the truth of God's Word and Spiritual principles are shared, and are received by faith, for others it is a journey over a longer period of time.

As you work with them, be watchful of some unspoken signals, such as: hanging their heads in shame, a stooped stance, clenched fists, uncontrolled shaking, writhing snake-like over the floor, eyes darting, etc. As you lean on the Holy Spirit for help, He will quicken your spiritual senses. Just as we have five physical senses; sight, sound, touch, taste, and smell, when we are born of the Spirit, our spiritual senses are sharpened.

Here are a few examples of what I have experienced:

**Sight:** I have seen people stand up and sit down again, yet physically they have not left their chair!

**Sound:** If there is demonic oppression, sometimes their voices change and become harsh, even for a moment.

**Touch:** On occasion, I have been overwhelmed with grief as I have felt the pain of individuals as they have walked in through the door.

**Taste:** I am becoming more able to identify those who are hungering after freedom.

**Smell:** Bad odours, not just body odours, could mean demons are present. When they are actively present, some of them seem to smell like burning sulphur or rotten eggs.

Not all people have deep wounds from the past that need healing. Many have simply lost their cutting edge. Some of the statements I have heard are:

- "We were getting on amazingly until about three months ago and now we just don't seem to agree on anything."

- "My walk with the Lord has been incredible but over the last year I feel as if I have been going through a desert, I don't seem to be able to hear from God."
- "I've been having nightmares for the last week and am scared of going to sleep!"
- "Over the last couple of months, I've been feeling down and don't know what's caused it."
- "I've been struggling with depression for years, but don't know what's triggered it."

A simple enquiry asking what circumstances or events may have led to them feeling this way, often reveals the trigger to their struggles. Many end-up blaming the devil for times such as these but we cannot blame the devil for everything. According to their response, it often becomes clear that they have compromised in one area or another, made wrong choices, or are holding someone or themselves in unforgiveness etc. I find that leading them through Scriptural principles is the key to helping them find their cutting edge again. A simple prayer of confession is generally all that's required and if they are comfortable with reading the Bible aloud in my presence, I will often ask them to read from their own translation of the Bible the Scriptures that the Holy Spirit brings to mind. These Scriptures are ones that I ask them to read when they need to forgive someone:

> *If we confess our sins, He is faithful and just to forgive us our sins and to cleanse us from all unrighteousness.*
>
> 1 JOHN 1:9 NKJV

*For if you forgive men when they sin against you, your heavenly Father will also forgive you. But if you do not forgive men their sins, your Father will not forgive your sins.*

MATTHEW 6:14–15 NIV

Indicate to them that forgiveness CAN be an event but it's usually a process, because certain things will trigger a remembrance of the hurt. If they are ready, they will need to repent of their sin of holding people in unforgiveness, then pray forgiving those who have hurt them, because you cannot pray these prayers on their behalf. Encourage them to pray aloud as there is great power when two or more agree, and you will both be making a proclamation into the heavenly realm. In some cases, they may need to make restitution for the wrong responses they have made in given situations (Matthew 5:23–24).

*Chapter 3*
# Contributing Factors to Emotional or Mental Struggles

Here are a few basic questions that might help highlight some possible causes of their emotional or mental struggles:

## A. Are you getting enough sleep?

Some people can cope with a few hours of sleep at night whereas others need a good eight hours or more. Be aware that regular over-sleeping can be a sign of depression. If you are concerned that the amount of sleep they need is excessive, or seriously lacking, ask them to see their doctor for a checkup. Shift workers often struggle emotionally when their shifts change from nights to days; it takes a while before their 'body clock' adjusts. Lack of sleep can really challenge their coping mechanisms!

## B. Is your lifestyle too hectic?

I might do a weekly planner with them to see what activities crowd out each day of the week. I might then challenge them to reduce some of their involvements and possibly consider changing jobs depending on what is triggering their frantic lifestyle. Some Christians seem to have the idea that the more hectic their church involvement is, the more spiritual they are. The devil can drive us to extremes, even in the church! We all need time to rest and play. If we don't take time to "come apart", we fall apart.

> *Then, because so many people were coming and going that they did not even have a chance to eat, he said to them, "Come with me by yourselves to a quiet place and get some rest."*
>
> MARK 6:31 NIV

## C. Are you eating properly?

In many cases, when problems arise, good eating habits fly out of the window! Eating disorders, such as comfort-eating, anorexia, and bulimia, are often triggered by wrong peer or work influences, serious mental, emotional, physical, or sexual abuse, or a need to have some kind of control in a chaotic world. This may result in their metabolism slowing down, their body resistance being lowered and them becoming prone to sickness and depression.

> *… do you not know that your body is the temple of the Holy Spirit who is in you, whom you have from God, and you are not your own? For you were bought at a price; therefore glorify God in your body and in your spirit, which are God's.*
>
> 1 CORINTHIANS 6:19–20 NKJV

I will encourage them to take responsibility for eating sensibly because in doing so, they are co-operating with God for the healing of their bodies. This can be quite a journey for those with eating disorders, and they will need a lot of encouragement. They may need professional help to overcome this, so do not be too proud to refer them.

## D. Have you had a medical check?

If they are feeling depressed, I will ask if they have seen their GP because certain medical conditions can trigger depression. I will ask if they are taking any prescription medicines, and if they are I tell them make sure they continue taking them until they feel they need to review them with their GP. When freedom and healing come from within, I encourage them to present themselves to their doctor for a review of their medication.

## E. How are you getting on at work?

Many people end up depressed because their job is soul destroying. If that is the case, find out what they are passionate about and what they are doing towards developing that passion. Connecting with a job they are passionate about and getting paid to do it is the best form of employment they can undertake because it brings satisfaction and great joy to the soul.

If there seems to be no obvious contributing factor, I will often draw these three diagrams:

This circle shows what and whom they are involved in, and the cross outside of the circle represents Christ's position in their lives.

Most people I see clearly indicate Christ as being inside their lives and freely admit that self is on the throne. They also admit that the relationships and activities they are involved in are somewhat chaotic.

When I draw this this second diagram, it becomes clear to them that they need to surrender control of their lives to Christ.

When I draw this third circle, many of them ask the Lord for forgiveness and ask Him to take control of their lives, while also asking Him to give them wisdom for the way forward so that their lives will be ordered of Him.

*The steps of a good man*
*are ordered by the Lord,*
*And He delights in his way.*
          PSALM 37:23 NKJV

Chapter 9
# How to Encourage them to Share

Some people come knowing exactly what it is they need help with. The shortest time I spent with someone was 20 minutes! This person just needed a listening ear and someone to agree in prayer with them during a time of confession.

> *Therefore confess your sins to each other and pray for each other so that you may be healed. The prayer of a righteous person is powerful and effective.*
>
> JAMES 5:16 NIV

For others, trying to get them to open-up can be as challenging as trying to open a can of beans without a can-opener. If people have been badly hurt in the past, whether physically, emotionally, mentally, sexually, or spiritually, it may take time for them to feel they can trust you with their deepest struggles. Once they feel they can trust you, they will open-up a lot more.

I might ask, "What would you like God to do for you?" This quite often breaks any tension they may be experiencing, and on many occasions, I have seen them become vulnerable and tearful. Handle your response sensitively or they will clam up and may even decide to leave. I often proceed by saying, "Let's pray,' then I ask the Lord to bring wholeness and healing to the person and invite the Holy Spirit to bring revelation for the way forward.

It is essential to be totally un-shockable when people start sharing their lives with you, because if they sense you are shocked or horrified by what they are telling you, they will lose trust in you and will want to leave.

> *Judge not, that you be not judged. For with what judgement you judge, you will be judged; and with the measure you use, it will be measured back to you.*
>
> MATTHEW 7:1–2 NKJV

The battle shifts up a gear here because, in many cases, the enemy has kept Christians bound with guilt and shame for years. The devil does not want them to be set free because they will become a threat to his kingdom, so authoritative prayer is needed here. Depending on their understanding of spiritual warfare, I may pray a silent prayer for them to receive a spirit of revelation but if they are open and receptive, I will pray for them audibly.

If at this point you feel totally out of your league, do not be too proud to admit it, and then refer them to someone else. But whatever you do, do not jump in with your own 'clever ideas', or judgemental attitude, and definitely do not give a super-spiritual response! Listen to the prompting of the Holy Spirit because He will more than likely quicken a Scripture to your heart in order to highlight principles that have been violated by them, or that need to be adhered to. Wait on Him for the right timing to see if He even wants you to share the verse with the person you are working with. Some spiritual insights received from the Holy Spirit may be revealed to you so that you know how to proceed but are not for sharing with the person at that time. The Lord has shown me pictures of situations they have been involved in, or He has given me strong impressions. On occasion, I have felt their deep pain or even grief.

Each person's situation is unique, therefore, I do not always use what is written in this book in the exact order that it is written. In some cases, I use the bulk of the diagrams and handouts mentioned, but in other cases, only a few. I wait on the Lord to show me whatever it is that seems appropriate at the time.

One of the easiest tools I use is my diagram of John 10:10, because they need to understand that they are experiencing a spiritual battle.

These drawings of a stick man in prison and a stick man free are often enough for them to show me where they see themselves now, and where they want to be.

> *The thief comes only to steal and kill and destroy; I have come that they may have life, and have it to the full.*
>
> JOHN 10:10 NIV

The Lord primarily speaks to us through His Word and through the inner witness of the Holy Spirit in our lives. He also speaks to us through the preaching of His Word as directed by the Holy Spirit. Christian media also plays a role in this, as does godly counsel. God can even use non-believers as a means of getting a word of encouragement or warning across to us!

Whereas there are many good voices out there in the world; voices of encouragement, etc., we are influenced and programmed over the years by so many negative voices. Many may have the intention of being well-meaning voices, but many voices may be quite destructive. A lot depends on the company we keep and the voices we've been listening to and believing?

Here are some examples of these VOICES:

The world: Family, friends, relatives, TV, internet, social media, books, magazines, workmates, etc.

The flesh: I call the flesh, I, Me, and Myself. These are my own selfish desires and choices, even when I know I should not be following them.

The devil: He uses our weaknesses and sometimes even our strengths against us. I believe he does this by whispering ungodly suggestions into our ears, etc., or even trying to drive us into over-commitment at home, at work, or even at church.

Here are some of the messages that they may have received from those negative voices over the years; many of which they have come to believe about themselves. I then hand them a list of some of these typical messages and ask them to tick off ones that are relevant to them. I reassure them that I am not going to mark them. Some people tick a few because that is what they believe about themselves, others, however, tick off the bulk of them.

## Messages

1. You're useless
2. I'm inferior
3. I'm not good enough to be loved
4. It's awful when things go wrong
5. Strong people don't ask for help
6. Making mistakes is terrible
7. My childhood will always affect me
8. People will always let me down
9. I should never upset anybody
10. If people cared for me, they'd know what I want
11. People must love me if I am to feel good about myself
12. I can't change what I think
13. You have no talents
14. You're stupid
15. People don't like me
16. You will never be any good
17. I ought to do better … I ought to do better
18. I deserved to be punished for my mistakes
19. I'm uninteresting
20. People ought to follow the advice I give
21. I can't stand it if people don't like me
22. People are not to be trusted
23. I must never show weakness
24. It is better to keep my thoughts to myself
25. I must always do everything perfectly or I will not be good enough

I reassure them that none of these are messages are ones their Heavenly Father speaks to them. This list of sentences they have ticked, usually shows me very clearly what the next step is that I need to use in order to show them the way to freedom in Christ.

## *Chapter 5*
# Genogram

If they have no clue as to why they are struggling, I will often ask them how long they have been feeling this way. Many indicate a specific time when things started to change, so I will ask them what happened at that time. This often triggers an emotional response, so be very sensitive here and give them time to express their emotions.

Some people find it very hard to pinpoint a time or event that triggered their negative feelings. In which case, I will suggest doing a Genogram. I tell them it is a bit like doing a Family Tree, but one that also encompasses much more than just their family. This is a particularly helpful tool if the person has been struggling since childhood, and it gives me a good framework to work from. Without a Genogram, it is easy to go around and around in circles or get easily distracted from the real issues. Obviously, it only works if the people are honest and open with you; I have found most people to be honest and open. I reassure them that these are just names, most of whom I will never get to meet, and the few I do know will never hear anything that's shared between us, unless of course there is a legal reason for me to do so.

### Practical 'How To's' on Doing a Genogram

Give them a sheet of white bond paper, a pen and something firm to lean on.

Have the paper in a 'Landscape' position and ask them to write their name in the middle of the paper. Either side of their name, they can add the names of their siblings: biological or stepbrothers and stepsisters. If they live in a blended family, ask them to include the other children's names. Indicating their age differences can often highlight some important information. Interestingly, the eldest child often has a bit of a tough time because they are cutting ground. Parenthood is new for Mum and Dad, and they make a lot of mistakes, quite often at the child's expense, even though unintentionally.

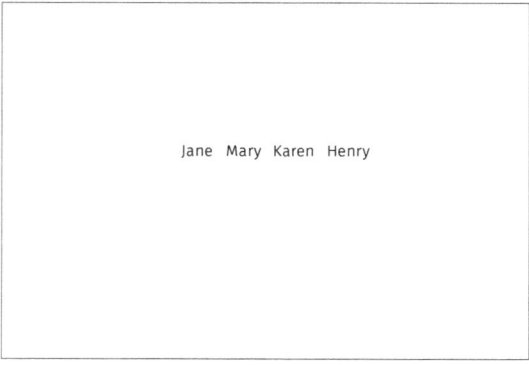

If one of the children is very bright academically, the other children often feel like failures. The youngest child often gets away with a lot, and some parents hang on to them too tightly so they end up feeling smothered. Each child is unique and when working with more than one child in the same family, you might wonder if they belong to the same family because their perceptions and experiences are so different.

In the space above their name, ask them to add names of their biological or foster parents, then grandparents on their mother's side and on their father's side. It is also important for them to write the names of parents or grandparents who have died, especially if they have had a strong influence on the family. Then add aunts, uncles, cousins and any close friends of mum or dad that spent a lot of time with their family.

In the space below their names, ask them to write names of childhood friends or enemies going back to their earliest remembrance. You are looking for key influential people in their lives; good, bad, or ugly! These might be teachers, fellow students, friends on the street, at school, sports teams, interest groups, tutors, etc., at college or university and colleagues or work. Include Church influences too, as sadly, I have seen a lot of people who have suffered because of abuse from church workers, clergy or their families.

If they are married, ask them to also include their marriage partner's name, in-laws (or outlaws!) and other family members, ex-wives/husbands, previous girlfriends, or boyfriends, especially if they have been sexually active. And last, but not least, ask if they have had any involvement in supernatural activities such as palm reading, horoscopes, Ouija Boards, tarot cards, séances etc., plus addictions of any kind, including over-the-counter medications, cigarettes, drugs or alcohol.

I have had people use the other side of the paper as well because they have very large families, or they have had a lot of social interaction in their life.

Their Genogram might end up looking something like this:

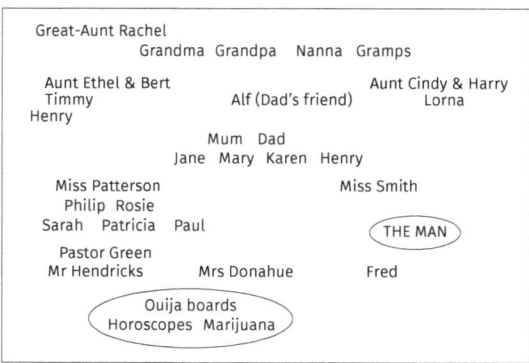

A crowded Genogram may indicate a lot of social interaction with their family and friends, etc., but I've had some Genograms with very few names on them, which may indicate a very closed, or overly private family. It may indicate an abusive or alcoholic family, in which case family members often end up not inviting people around so that they can keep the truth hidden. Yet quite often, when they are in public or at church, they seem to be a very friendly, positive family.

Even watching them fill their Genogram in can tell you a lot. Some will highlight names of people who have hurt them by scribbling heavily under their names. Just keep note of any observations you make because you may need to refer to them later.

Here are some other key questions that you might consider asking while they are filling up their Genogram:

1. Were they brought up in a city, town, village, or out in the country?
2. Were they day scholars or boarders?

3. What was their dad's profession? If their parents have moved home frequently, children often choose not to make close friends because parting is painful.
4. Did they have a working mother or a stay-at-home mum?
5. How did the family manage financially?
6. It's also important to find out if their parents, grandparents, or great-grandparents have been involved in secret orders such as Freemasonry, or if they have been involved in witchcraft, etc., because these generational ties also need to be broken.

Make a note of any relevant information given in response to these questions. By the time they have completed the Genogram, they might need a short break, a cup of tea or a glass of water. Reassure them that they are doing well and that they are making good progress.

After completing the Genogram, they may choose to stop until their next appointment, as it may trigger off quite a few emotions and unlock a lot of pain. Be very sensitive here.

If they are ready to continue, tell them that you would now like them to categorise their Genogram into three categories by underlining each name with one of three kinds of red line:

1. A straight line ——— for people who have mostly had a positive influence on their lives.
2. A wavy line ⌒⌒ for people who have given them a bit of grief but who have also been quite positive.
3. A zigzag wwww for the ones who have caused a lot of pain: verbally, mentally, emotionally, physically, or sexually.

And lastly, it is also important that they put a line under their own name as well, as a lot of people struggle with themselves.

I will not usually spend longer than 1½–2 hours on one session as they get quite tired. If by the time you get to the Genogram you've already taken an hour and a half, reassure them that they are making good progress and tell them you'll see them again another day, preferably within a week's time. Remind them that the names on the sheet of paper are just names to you, but they are important names to them and to God. Reiterate that you will keep these notes in a safe place until you see them next.

Encourage them to read through the Scriptures and look over the diagrams you have given them before their next visit. Indicate to them that the battle in the heavenly realm may intensify because they want to get serious about their relationship with God. Explain to them that the devil does not want them to be free because he knows they will positively impact their world so much more once freedom in Christ is theirs. Then pray for them before they leave.

*Chapter 6*

# Do they have any idea of the War Zone they are in?

Before progressing any further with the Genogram, I prefer to give some Scriptural teaching here. It is vital that the people you see have a basic understanding of how things operate in the spiritual realm because with greater understanding comes greater freedom.

When we are born again our spirits are born of the Spirit of God, but our souls need a lot of sanctifying. Most of us have received a lot of wrong programming over the years but quite a lot of this wrong programming falls away almost immediately when we are born-again, whereas other areas take time for our minds to be renewed.

People who work with computers talk about 'GIGO': Garbage In, Garbage Out! There is a Scriptural principle regarding this.

> *The good man brings good things out of the good stored up in his heart, and the evil man brings evil things out of the evil stored up in his heart. For out of the overflow of his heart his mouth speaks.*
> LUKE 6:45 NIV

Most Christians have no idea about the intensity of the battle. They only see the battle against people and situations and not the battle in the spiritual realm. Once they begin to understand and see why the battle rages, they start understanding how Satan uses people to do his work for him, including how Satan uses even them, often in their ignorance, to do his work.

I generally start with Genesis 1:26–28 to give them God's original mandate for man.

> *Then God said, "Let us make man in our image, in our likeness, and let them rule over the fish of the sea and the birds of the air, over the livestock, over all the earth, and over all the creatures that move along the ground." So God created man in his own image, in the image of God he created him; male and female he created them. God blessed them and said to them, "Be fruitful and increase in number; fill the earth and subdue it. Rule over the fish of the sea and the birds of the air and over every living creature that moves on the ground."*
>
> GENESIS 1:26–28 NIV

We have been given the mandate to rule and to reign. I then share about the war in heaven and the fall of Lucifer.

If they feel comfortable reading Scripture aloud, I will ask them to read this passage from the King James Version:

(I will read it if they do not feel comfortable)

> *The Fall of Lucifer*
>
> *How you are fallen from heaven,*
>
> *O Lucifer, son of the morning! How you are cut down to the ground, You who weakened the nations!*
>
> *For you have said in your heart:*

> *"I will ascend into heaven, I will exalt my throne above the stars of God; I will also sit on the mount of the congregation On the farthest sides of the north;*
>
> *I will ascend above the heights of the clouds,*
>
> *I will be like the Most High."*
>
> *Yet you shall be brought down to Sheol,*
>
> *To the lowest depths of the Pit.*
>
> ISAIAH 14:12–15 NKJV

By the time they have read this passage they can usually see why the battle rages here on earth. The devil had no authority over mankind until after the Fall. I then lead them to Genesis 3:1–13 and ask them to read what happened during the Fall of Man. I then explain to them that by listening to and responding to Satan's subtle lies, Adam and Eve handed over their God-given authority to Satan and reacted in typical fashion when questioned by God. The man blamed God, "The woman you put here with me—she gave me some fruit from the tree, and I ate it," the woman blamed the serpent, and the serpent didn't have a leg to stand on! Shame, guilt, and fear set in, and these became barriers between man and God. Adam and Eve did not die physically but their spiritual relationship with God was broken that day.

One of the greatest blessings God has given us is freedom of choice and yet, in this case, it became mankind's greatest curse. We all have this same freedom of choice today, but we also have a very real enemy who wants to keep us away from experiencing God's best in our lives.

When Satan was cast out of heaven along with his demons (fallen angels), he knew he was no match for God. When an earthly man knows he has met his match with another man, he will often go after the other man's wife and kids to retaliate. We are both God's bride and His children, so we become Satan's target. I sincerely believe that Satan strikes us because we, knowingly or unknowingly, end up as the only weapon he has against God.

Many Christians do not have a clear understanding of these two kingdoms in operation:

1. The kingdom of darkness – Satan's kingdom
2. The Kingdom of Light – God's Kingdom

> *Finally, my brethren, be strong in the Lord and in the power of His might. Put on the whole armor of God, that you may be able to stand against the wiles of the devil. For we do not wrestle against flesh and blood, but against principalities, against powers, against the rulers of the darkness of this age, against spiritual hosts of wickedness in the heavenly places.*
>
> EPHESIANS 6:10–12 NKJV

When I hold up their Genogram with all its wavy lines and zigzags, they begin to understand why they have struggled for so long. I remind them that it's not the people on the Genogram that they have been struggling against but the devil and his demons, and that he's more than likely still using those very people to cause them pain. Satan also delights in using us to do his dirty work!

Yes, some of their pain has been because of their own blatant disobedience and they are reaping the effects of it, but restoration is available. They are not out of the woods yet, but frequently by this stage, they have a glimmer of hope and some even anticipate the way out.

*Chapter 7*
# How to Work Through Their Genogram

When they are ready to continue working through the Genogram, start with the straight lines under the good people's names. Ask them if they have ever given thanks to the Lord for these people. Many people I have seen had not even realised that there were any good people in their lives. Some have responded quite emotionally at this point because all they had seen was pain, and that is all they had focussed on. I encourage them to pray aloud and give thanks to God for the good people. I also remind them that in doing so, they are making a positive proclamation into the spiritual realm. As they pray, I also pray in agreement with them, which is very powerful (Matthew 18:19). They might pray for them as a complete group of good people, but many will give special thanks for specific individuals who have impacted their lives positively.

Give them the freedom to pray as they feel led. As they pray giving thanks, they are engaging in warfare by making positive proclamations into the heavenly realms.

I have had a few people who have never prayed aloud before and certainly not in company. I then offer to start them off by praying simple sentence prayers that they repeat. Usually after one or two sentences, they begin to form their own prayers. I have only had one person who has refused point blank to pray aloud. Encourage these people to pray silently anyway. This is challenging, because you can't agree with their prayer, so more grace needs to be exercised here.

I usually give them a bit of homework by encouraging them to thank the good people for their positive influence in their lives, either by phone, email, or when sending Birthday or Christmas cards, etc. It releases blessing upon the hearer and affirms again that God has had key positive people on hand, even during their pain and confusion.

Please remember that each person is unique. Use whatever tool comes to mind and is appropriate for that time. DO NOT be bent on going through everything written here. Allow the Holy Spirit to lead you or you will end up with a neat 'formula', which may or may not work and, in some cases, you may end up causing more confusion for them.

It is vital to remember at this stage that you must proceed at their speed, or they will pray prayers of confession and forgiveness just to get you off their backs! I have had some who want to go away and think about what they have been taught, because they want to check the Scriptures out for themselves first before they come back. Some phone a few days later and are so desperate to be set free, that they want to come back again sooner. You may even have one or two who decide not to come back. Be gracious with them, and do not forget, the choice is theirs. All you can do is show them the way to freedom, but they have to take a step of faith to receive it. Some struggle with the whole 'faith issue' at this stage. I might ask them if they are born again, and when they respond positively, I ask them, "How do you know?" This usually is enough for them to understand what faith is.

Quite often, at this time you may become very aware that the battle is raging intensely. The enemy has kept them locked into their pain for so long he does not want to let them go. Sometimes I will ask, "How desperate are you to be set free?" This quite often is all they need to make the choice to lay it all down at the foot of the cross.

It is important for them to know that they will have to do the praying because you cannot pray these prayers on their behalf. Remind them that you are going to be praying in agreement with them because there is great power when two or more agree (Matthew 18:19).

The wavy lines under names of people on their Genogram may trigger a few emotions when it is time to pray. Be very sensitive here. Maybe ask them about some of the good things these people have done that have impacted their lives and, if they are open and ready, ask them to give thanks to God for the good impact they have had on their lives. However, there will also be certain things they will need to forgive the wavy line people for.

Some people you see may not understand why **they** need to forgive the ones who have hurt them. Sensitively remind them that they have been holding these people in unforgiveness and that is why they are struggling. Some may tell you they feel justified in feeling the way they do, so remind them that that person is answerable to God for their wrong actions and will have to give an account to Him one day. At this point, I often turn to 1 John 1:9 and the Lord's Prayer (Matthew 6:9–13), which most Christians are familiar with, but I also include verses 14–15 because it says, *"For if you forgive men their trespasses, your heavenly*

*Father will also forgive you. ¹⁵ But if you do not forgive men their trespasses, neither will your Father forgive your trespasses."* I then ask them about some of their wrong responses to these people and most of the time they openly admit them.

When they are ready to pray, this must be approached from two aspects:

1. They need to forgive and release those who have caused them pain.
2. They need to ask God to forgive them for all the wrongs that they have done. This includes their wrong thoughts and responses to those who have caused them pain.

Remind them that forgiveness is a choice. Usually, by this time, they are ready to ask the Lord for forgiveness for their wrong responses and to release these people to the Lord. Because forgiveness is more often than not a process rather than an event, we talk about different 'buttons' the enemy presses to trigger negative responses. They usually know exactly which 'buttons' some of these folks press that trigger an unforgiving or angry attitude. I then lead them to Matthew 18:21–35 NIV.

> *Then Peter came to Jesus and asked, "Lord, how many times shall I forgive my brother when he sins against me? Up to seven times?"*
>
> *Jesus answered, "I tell you, not seven times, but seventy-seven times. "Therefore, the kingdom of heaven is like a king who wanted to settle accounts with his servants. As he began the settlement, a man who owed him ten thousand talents was brought to him. Since he was not able to pay, the master ordered that he and his wife and his children and all that he had be sold to repay the debt.*

> "At this the servant fell on his knees before him. 'Be patient with me,' he begged, 'and I will pay back everything.' The servant's master took pity on him, canceled the debt and let him go.
>
> "But when that servant went out, he found one of his fellow servants who owed him a hundred denari. He grabbed him and began to choke him. 'Pay back what you owe me!' he demanded.
>
> "His fellow servant fell to his knees and begged him, 'Be patient with me, and I will pay it back.'
>
> "But he refused. Instead, he went off and had the man thrown into prison until he could pay the debt. When the other servants saw what had happened, they were greatly distressed and went and told their master everything that had happened.
>
> "Then the master called the servant in. 'You wicked servant,' he said, 'I canceled all that debt of yours because you begged me to. Shouldn't you have had mercy on your fellow servant just as I had on you?' In anger his master handed him over to the jailers to be tortured, until he should pay back all he owed.
>
> "This is how my heavenly Father will treat each of you unless you forgive your brother or sister from your heart."
>
> MATTHEW 18:21–35 NIV

The King James Version says, *"his lord was wroth and delivered him to the tormentors, till he should pay all that was due unto him."* It is important for them to understand that we are the ones who end up in torment of soul if we don't forgive (vs 32–35).

I have found that some people struggle the most to forgive themselves, but this is also a vital step they will need to take to receive freedom. (See diagram Condemnation or Conviction – Chapter 9.)

When you get to this point, share a word of encouragement with them because they are sharing deep issues with you that they have maybe never shared with anyone else before. Refer to my John 10:10 diagram (page 21) and remind them of the freedom that is available to them in Christ.

This may be a suitable time to stop before proceeding to the zigzag lines, especially if either you or they feel emotionally tired. Be sensitive to what the Holy Spirit is saying. Before they leave, pray, and give thanks for the progress they are making and pray the Lord's protection over them, along with a fresh filling of the Holy Spirit. Make an appointment to see them again in a few days or a week later.

You might find one or two people who refuse point blank to forgive the people with zigzag lines. Be sensitive to the fact that memories have been re-awakened; memories that may be triggering a lot of inner pain. At the end of the day, this is their choice but before they leave, thank them for sharing so honestly with you and remind them that you are there for them if they would like further help.

Before they leave, remind them that the battles in the heavenly realm may intensify because they want to get serious about their relationship with God. If they indicate that this makes them feel a bit anxious, ask them to read Colossians 2:13–15. The enemy has been disarmed even though he goes around like a roaring lion seeking whom he may devour (1 Peter 5:8). He has no teeth, which means he can only slobber or gum them to death if they allow him to.

*Chapter 8*
# Dealing with the Zigzags

After dealing with the wavy lines, many folks know and understand how they need to appropriate the truth of God's Word to receive further freedom and healing in Christ. Therefore, this often makes it so much easier to deal with the zigzags. But for some, their pain runs very deep. So be very sensitive to the leading of the Holy Spirit.

I quite often use the example of Jonah to highlight how we often suffer because of others' sins. I call this the Jonah Principle.

> *The word of the Lord came to Jonah son of Amittai: "Go to the great city of Nineveh and preach against it, because its wickedness has come up before me."*
>
> *But Jonah ran away from the Lord and headed for Tarshish. He went down to Joppa, where he found a ship bound for that port. After paying the fare, he went aboard and sailed for Tarshish to flee from the Lord.*
>
> *Then the Lord sent a great wind on the sea, and such a violent storm arose that the ship threatened to break up. All the sailors were afraid and each cried out to his own god. And they threw the cargo into the sea to lighten the ship.*
>
> *But Jonah had gone below deck, where he lay down and fell into a deep sleep.*
>
> JONAH 1:1–5 NIV

Due to Jonah's blatant disobedience, a terrifying storm arose that threatened to break up the ship, and the sailors were scared. They suffered because of another man's disobedience. The owner of the ship no doubt had serious repairs to do to restore the vessel. The cargo was thrown into the sea which meant that businessmen who had sent their cargo to Tarshish, ended up losing it all to the sea. They probably did not have insurance in those days. In the meantime, Jonah was fast asleep, totally oblivious to the different storms that were raging.

Over the years, I have seen many Christians who have suffered from fear, loss of identity, and torment of soul, due to them being victims of other people's sins. In most cases, this pain has been triggered by abuse; whether verbal, physical, emotional, mental, or sexual. Some abusers have even managed to convince their victims that they were the ones who triggered the abuse because of their "so-called" bad behaviour.

For people who have been affected for years because of other people's sins against them, I might then draw this diagram and ask them if they want to remain as victims or become agents for change:

Victim ........................... or ........................... Agent?

Use this very sensitively because it may give them the impression that you are making light of their pain.

Those who have caused them great anguish of soul are usually 'fast asleep', totally oblivious to the storm raging in their lives. It was only when the sailors threw Jonah overboard, that peace came (Jonah 1:15). I encourage them to do the same spiritually (not physically ... even though in many cases, that might be their preferred option!), and 'throw those people overboard' and let them go. In doing so, I have seen many folk experience freedom and the Lord's peace.

If you are not entirely sure of the authority you have in Jesus' Name, direct these folks to a senior Pastor or a born again Counsellor who can journey with them through the zig-zag lanes. This is very important at this stage, because I have had demons manifest themselves and I have heard them speak with harsh voices that are not the person's voice. Some folks have ended up writhing on the floor snake-like. If this happens, this is when you need to take up the authority that is rightfully yours in Christ (Luke 10:19) and command the demonic forces of evil to be gone, in the Name of Jesus.

Satan hates the Name of Jesus, the Word of God and the blood of the Lamb, and he also knows the difference between those who minister in Jesus' Name who have authority over him and his demons, and those who don't (Acts 19:13–16). Therefore, it is vital for you to know and understand the authority that is rightfully yours before you continue with these folks, or the demons will come and attack you!

In my experience, these manifestations have mostly occurred in people who have opened doors into the demonic realm via drugs, demonic TV series' and movies, Ouija boards, T.M, séances, palm reading, witchcraft, etc., which means that they'll not only need to forgive the people who have caused them grief in one way or another, but will also need to confess and renounce the demonic activities they have consciously or unwittingly opened the door to (Proverbs 28:13). See notes in Chapter 12 on Deliverance Ministry.

*Chapter 9*
# Possible Blockages in their Belief System

For some people, when they get to the zigzag lines, they seem to have a mental blockage regarding how they can be set free. This is often the time I share the ABC Principle of Emotion.

It is what we believe about ourselves that triggers our consequential emotions.

This is how it works for most of us:

**A = Activating Event:** This is something that happens to all of us which is beyond our power to control.

**B = Belief System:** This is what we believe about the situation.

**C = Consequent Emotion:** This is triggered according to our belief system.

**A** does not determine **C**, even though it may seem as if it does.

**B** determines **C**. It is how our belief system interprets the event that leads to positive or negative emotions.

For example:

**Activating Event:** "I've just heard from a mutual friend that my best friend is getting married."

**Belief System:** "I'm obviously not his/her best friend or I would have been told first."

**Consequent Emotion**: Jealousy, anger, disappointment, resentment.

Maybe something more traumatic might be:

**Activating Event:** "My Dad had sex with me regularly when I was a child and I didn't know anything was wrong until I entered puberty, because then he didn't want to have sex with me anymore."

**Belief System:** "Men are disgusting, and I'm only there to be used and abused." "There must be something wrong with me."

**Consequent Emotion:** Guilt, shame, fear, anger, resentment, despair

To show them how they can positively change their belief system. I then share **D** and **E** with them:

**D = Denounce the negative belief system:** "I'm justified in feeling angry, but not all men are disgusting, and no, there's nothing wrong with me, he's the one with the problem!"

### E = Exchange the negative belief system for the truth of God's Word:

> *Do not repay anyone evil for evil. Be careful to do what is right in the eyes of everybody. If it is possible, as far as it depends on you, live at peace with everyone. Do not take revenge, my dear friends, but leave room for God's wrath, for it is written: "It is mine to avenge; I will repay," says the Lord.*
>
> ROMANS 12:17–19 NIV

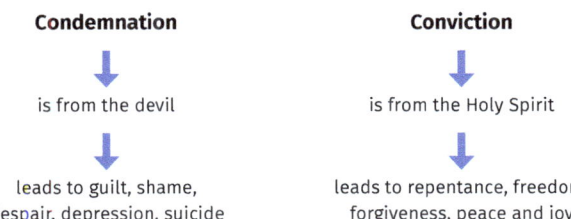

The devil delights in condemning us. Sadly, many Christians don't know the difference between condemnation and conviction, so I usually explain it to them with this diagram:

I frequently use Isaiah 61:1–3 here because it highlights the differences between the Kingdom of Darkness and the Kingdom of Light.

*The Spirit of the Sovereign LORD is on me,*
*because the LORD has anointed me*
*to preach good news to the poor.*
*He has sent me to bind up the broken-hearted,*
*to proclaim freedom for the captives*
*and release from darkness for the prisoners,*
*to proclaim the year of the*
*LORD's favor and the day of vengeance of our God,*
*to comfort all who mourn,*
*and provide for those who grieve in Zion—*
*to bestow on them a crown of beauty instead of ashes,*
*the oil of gladness instead of mourning,*
*and a garment of praise instead of a spirit of despair.*
*They will be called oaks of righteousness, a planting of the*
*LORD for the display of his splendour.*

ISAIAH 61:1–3 NIV

As they read the passage, I often write out the differences in these verses in two columns, see below:

| Kingdom of Darkness | Kingdom of Light |
| --- | --- |
| Broken-hearted | Healing |
| Captive | Freedom |
| Prisoner | Release |
| Mourning | Comfort |
| Ashes | Beauty |
| Sorrow | Joy |
| Despair | Praise |

Then I give them this list of Scriptures showing how God sees them:

## He Gives Me Security

| | |
| --- | --- |
| Romans 8:1–2 | I am free forever from condemnation |
| Romans 8:28 | I am assured that all things work together for good |
| Romans 8:35 | I cannot be separated from the love of God |
| 2 Corinthians 1:21–22 | I have been established, anointed and sealed by God |
| Colossians 3:3 | I am hidden with Christ in God |
| Philippians 1:6 | I am confident that the good work that God has begun in me will be perfected |
| Philippians 3:20 | I am a citizen of heaven |
| 2 Timothy 1:7 | I have not been given a spirit of fear but of power, love and a sound mind |
| Hebrews 4:16 | I can find grace and mercy in time of need |

| | |
|---|---|
| 1 John 5:18 | I am born of God, and the evil one cannot touch me |

## He Gives Me Significance

| | |
|---|---|
| Matthew 5:13–14 | I am the salt and light of the earth |
| John 15:1 and 5 | I am the branch of the true vine, a channel of His life |
| John 15:16 | I have been chosen and appointed to bear fruit |
| Acts 1:8 | I am Christ's personal witness |
| 1 Corinthians 3:16 | I am God's temple |
| 2 Corinthians 6:1 | I am God's co-worker |
| Ephesians 2:6 | I am seated with Christ in the heavenly realm |
| Ephesians 2:10 | I am God's workmanship |
| Ephesians 3:12 | I may approach God with freedom and confidence |
| Philippians 4:13 | I can do all things through Christ Who strengthens me |

## He Gives Me Self-worth

| | |
|---|---|
| John 1:12 | I am God's child |
| John 15:15 | I am Christ's friend |
| Romans 5:1 | I have been justified |
| 1 Corinthians 6:17 | I am united with the Lord and am one spirit with Him |
| 1 Corinthians 6:19–20 | I have been bought with a price, I belong to God |
| 1 Corinthians 12:27 | I am a member of Christ's body |
| Ephesians 1:1 | I am a saint |
| Ephesians 1:5 | I have been adopted as God's child |

| | |
|---|---|
| Ephesians 2:18 | I have direct access to God through the Holy Spirit |
| Colossians 1:14 | I have been redeemed and forgiven of all my sins |
| Colossians 2:10 | I am complete in Christ |

I will often ask them to read a few of these aloud and make some proclamations into the heavenly realms. Even as they make these proclamations, I have seen many come into a greater freedom and understanding of who they are in God, and many have been overwhelmed by these truths.

With some people, all it takes is one two-hour session to lead them to freedom. With others, it is quite a journey and may take a few sessions, or even months or years! Each person is unique, so work at their speed, not yours.

Chapter 10
# Different Areas of Need

We are tripartite beings, which means we are spiritual beings that have a soul, and we live in a physical body. So, in order to function well, all three areas need our attention.

> *Now may the God of peace Himself sanctify you completely; and may your whole spirit, soul and body be preserved blameless at the coming of our Lord Jesus Christ.*
>
> 1 THESSALONIANS 5:23 NKJV

These three areas of need can be illustrated in diagrammatic form as three concentric circles.

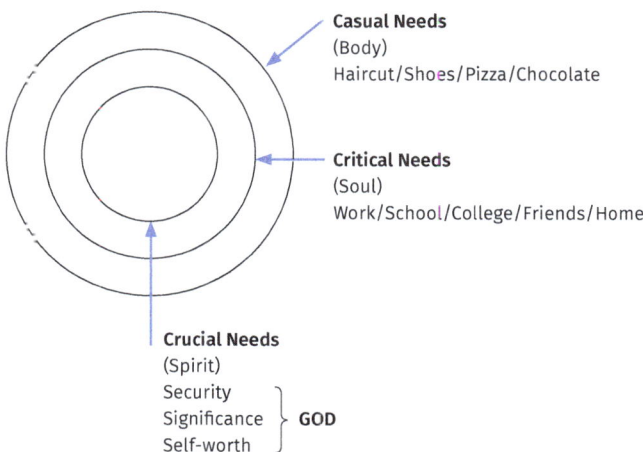

## 1. Casual needs

These affect our body and might include: a new pair of trainers, a new outfit, a haircut, pizza, a bar of chocolate, etc.

If we do not get these today or tomorrow, it generally doesn't cause much of a problem, except, perhaps, if you come from a family that has serious financial constraints.

## 2. Critical needs

These affect our soul (our mind, will, and emotions), and are to do with a good home environment, a good school/college/work environment and good relationships.

If there are challenges in any of these three key areas, they can cause a lot of pain and hardship. A few examples of these might be: we might lose our home due to loss of work; there might be an increase in the mortgage rate; a partner may die, or we may need to move to a different area to look after aging parents, etc.

We have, however, even deeper needs than these which we may or may not be consciously aware of. These are called crucial needs.

## 3. Crucial needs

These affect our spirits, because these needs are connected to our security, significance, and self-worth.

As children, our security, significance and self-worth are closely linked to those who brought us up. This is usually our parents, but it may have been stepparents, grandparents, aunts, foster parents, guardians, etc. We were totally dependent on them to provide us with security, significance, and self-worth while we were little.

In the natural progression of time, children learn to become independent of their parents or guardians. This is healthy and normal, but the greatest challenge comes when, as adults, we look to the critical areas of home, work, and relationships to satisfy our crucial needs for security, significance, and self-worth.

It is only when our security, significance and self-worth are in God, and God alone, that we receive inner peace and joy, even at times when we are experiencing pain and turmoil. This is the key difference between us and the rest of the world, because we have a quiet confidence and assurance of who we are in God. This becomes more evident as we spend time developing our relationship with Christ, and this totally confounds the world around us!

To bring greater understanding of how the Different Areas of Need; Voices; Wrong Messages; and the ABC Principle of Emotion fit together, I often use the Masterlife Cross[2] diagram because many people are visual learners. I have shown it in various stages, but it all ends up in one diagram. I talk them through it as I draw it.

---

2  © Copyright 1980, 1982, The Sunday School Board of the Southern Baptist Convention. All rights reserved.

## Step 1

I start by drawing a cross within an outer circle, because at some point in time everyone, whether believer or non-believer, is going to have to give a personal account to God for what they have done in life.

## Step 2

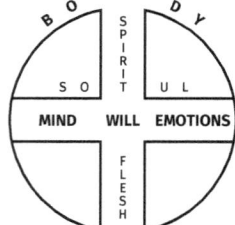

FLESH = I, ME & MYSELF

We are spiritual beings who have a soul, and we live in a physical body. I write SPIRIT down the top-centre of the cross and BODY along the top outer edge of the circle. I explain that 'body' includes flesh and blood, bones, skin, eyes, etc., I then write SOUL along the top centre edge of the cross bar and remind them that our soul is made up of our mind, will and emotions. I write these along the middle of the cross.

The Bible often speaks of the heart as the seat of our emotions and there are countless Scriptures that indicate the heart as having intellect, thought, emotion, character, love, compassion, and faithfulness (Matthew 5:8; Hebrews 4:12; Proverbs 3:5–6; Psalm 51:10; Jeremiah 17:9–10).

Scripture also talks about us having the mind of the flesh (Romans 8:6), which is often referred to as our sinful, carnal nature, or Adamic nature. I write FLESH down the bottom-centre of the cross, and I call the flesh, I, Me and Myself.

There is a story of a man who had two fighting dogs. People would bet on either of the dogs before they engaged in a fight. The owner also bet on one of the dogs and won every time. When other punters observed this, they asked him how he knew which dog would win the fight. He answered, "The one I fed."

What are the people you see feeding? The flesh or the spirit? What they feed will determine how they respond. Their emotions are determined by their belief system and the choices they make. This is the ABC Principle of Emotion in action. On the diagram their Will sits between the spirit and the flesh, and this is where the battle rages.

There is no instant formula in this regard, as it comes at differing speeds with each person, but slowly, as they grasp the truth of God's Word and apply it in their lives, freedom and healing is theirs.

## Step 3

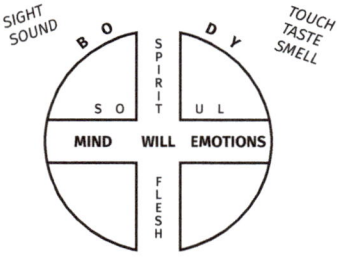

Messages are primarily received through the five senses: sight, sound, touch, taste, and smell. In whatever way these messages are received, they often trigger memories: good, bad, or ugly. These are dealt with in greater detail through the ABC Principle of Emotion.

## Step 4

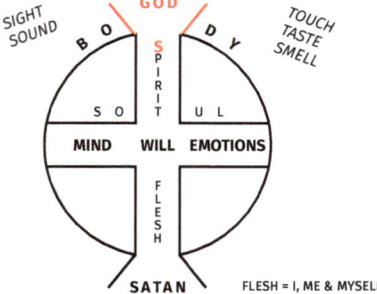

From the time they were born-again, or born of the Spirit of God, the Holy Spirit came to indwell them. I indicate this on the diagram by drawing a red S over the small 's' of their spirit and then draw lines flowing upwards to indicate the doorway to

God as being open, giving immediate access to the power and presence of the Holy Spirit at work in their lives.

## Step 5

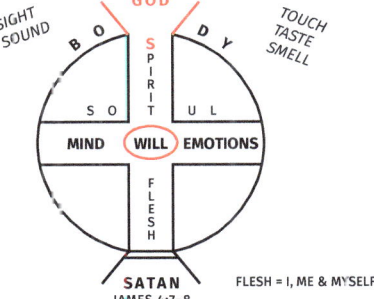

Because the flesh is greatly influenced by the voices of the world, and the devil, we are tempted to go against what the Holy Spirit, our conscience, and our moral values tell us.

We wrestle not against flesh and blood but principalities and powers in the spiritual realm (Ephesians 6:10–12), so I also draw lines flowing downwards from the flesh to indicate Satan's luring influence on their carnal nature, and this is where their greatest challenge takes place.

I draw a red circle around the word WILL, because it is a choice they will need to make to either follow the way of the flesh or the way of the Holy Spirit who indwells them. I also draw two lines just above the word Satan to indicate how the door to the devil closes each time they pray, worship the Lord, repent of listening to the devil's lies, and walk in obedience to the voice of the Holy Spirit.

James 4:7–8 is the Scripture I use to show them how to overcome Satan's schemes.

> *⁷ Submit yourselves, then, to God. Resist the devil, and he will flee from you. ⁸ Come near to God and he will come near to you. Wash your hands, you sinners, and purify your hearts, you double-minded.*
>
> JAMES 4:7–8 NIV

Drawing near to God and walking in obedience to Him is a journey we are all on, and the more consciously aware we are of God's presence and His desire to help us walk in victory moment by moment, day by day, the greater the strength, authority, and determination we will have to resist and overcome Satan's ploys.

Each time we give in to the devil's temptations or succumb to guilt and shame, he spiritually cripples us and renders us ineffective for the Kingdom of God. The devil delights in this because, in effect, we end up doing his work: putting ourselves down, self-harming, being critical of others etc. This is often the time that I remind them of the drawing of a stick man in prison and a stick man free, and this usually highlights to them where they are and where they want to be.

The irony of it all is: when they forgive those that have caused them pain, THEY are set free! (John 8:31–32)

Listen carefully to the voice of the Holy Spirit. God knows everything about the person and longs to see them set free. Nothing is hidden from Him, and He can quicken any of the gifts of the Spirit to you that are required for each situation. For example, He might give you a word of knowledge regarding something that has not been shared. Whenever I receive something like this, I will usually ask the person for permission before sharing it, especially if it is of a sensitive nature. I might phrase it like this, "I'm getting a strong impression of something, would you mind if I share it?" The Lord gave me a word of knowledge when I was listening to a young lady who had been struggling with eating disorders. The Holy Spirit showed me that she had been sexually abused as a child but had been too ashamed to share it. When she gave me permission to share what I felt, she burst into tears because she had never shared this with anyone, and that day she received freedom and restoration.

You may have never received a 'word of knowledge' before but do not limit what God can do in and through you. The best spiritual gift you can receive is that which is needed at the time.

*Now about spiritual gifts, brothers, I do not want you to be ignorant… There are different kinds of gifts, but the same Spirit … Now to each one the manifestation of the Spirit is given for the common good … and he gives them to each one, just as he determines.*

1 CORINTHIANS 12:1–11 NIV

## Chapter 11
# A Few Examples

At one time, a precious old lady in one of our congregations was due to fly to India to see an old friend of hers. She was anxious about going because she had a nasty skin condition, known as psoriasis, on her feet. She came asking for prayer because she was anxious about going to India with that condition. God stirred up faith within our prayer group to believe for her healing. We prayed for her once a week over a four-week period, coming against the spirit of fear, and claiming God's promise in 2 Timothy 1:7 for her, and the Lord healed her.

*For God has not given us a spirit of fear, but of power and of love and of a sound mind.*

2 TIMOTHY 1:7 NKJV

I have also seen physical healing take place once pain from the past has been dealt with.

The human brain is complex, and we subconsciously find ways to cope with our pain. We may try and hide it with alcohol, pornography or drugs, bury it, 'stuff it into a box' or pretend it's not there, but at some point in life, a seemingly insignificant trigger may result in a response that is totally disproportionate to the situation.

With some who have been sexually abused for example, it might only affect them when they get married because they struggle to respond sexually to their spouse. With others, it might only be when their own children reach the age that they were when they were abused physically, mentally, emotionally or sexually, that a response is triggered.

Here is an example of this: During a time of prayer at a Bible Study I was leading, one mum was struggling with the fact that her child was starting Primary School and had to go to boarding school because they lived too far away from it to take her every day. Her response was totally out of proportion to the usual mum struggling to let her child become more independent of her.

When we asked about her own experience of school, she totally lost it! Amid sobs of anger and pain, she recounted an experience she had had as a little girl at school. As a young child she also started boarding school, and at that time she had the most beautiful, long red hair. During the night, while she was asleep, some girls came with a pair of scissors and cut her hair short. She was devastated, and buried this pain for years, but in the meantime, she had developed a relational style of anger to protect herself. When we showed her the passage from Matthew 18:21–35, she realised what she had done. She had held those girls in unforgiveness for all those years. However, that day, she chose to ask the Lord for forgiveness, and she forgave those girls. In doing so she was set free. It was an amazing release, and an incredible transformation in her character took place!

Some people get locked into any of these: depression, anger, shyness, work, alcohol, drugs, promiscuity, homosexuality, self-harm, eating disorders, joining street gangs, etc., to help cope with their pain. They may see them as 'safe zones' because they seem to bring a measure of temporary relief, but this behaviour clearly indicates that there is a deeper root that needs dealing with.

I have seen a few who have been locked in grief for years because a parent or another person who abused them died without any restoration having first taken place. After working with them through the stages of grief and using Scriptural principles regarding the importance of forgiveness, and the consequences of unforgiveness, many have received freedom. Watching the Holy Spirit at work while they receive and apply the truth of God's Word is nothing short of miraculous. It confirms what Paul says in Romans 12:

> *¹Therefore I urge you, brothers and sisters, by the mercies of God, to present your bodies [dedicating all of yourselves, set apart] as a living sacrifice, holy and well-pleasing to God, which is your rational (logical, intelligent) act of worship. ²And do not be conformed to this world [any longer with its superficial values and customs], but be transformed and progressively changed [as you mature spiritually] by the renewing of your mind [focusing on godly values and ethical attitudes], so that you may prove [for yourselves] what the will of God is, that which is good and acceptable and perfect [in His plan and purpose for you].*
>
> ROMANS 12:1–2 AMPLIFIED BIBLE

It is important to understand why people do what they do. It will help us see them through Jesus' eyes. Jesus looked beyond their outward appearance and behaviour to their cry within so that He could bring them healing, forgiveness and restoration.

> *The teachers of the law and the Pharisees brought in a woman caught in adultery. They made her stand before the group and said to Jesus, "Teacher, this woman was caught in the act of adultery. In the Law Moses commanded us to stone such women. Now what do you say?" They were using this question as a trap, in order to have a basis for accusing him.*
>
> *But Jesus bent down and started to write on the ground with his finger. When they kept on questioning him, he straightened up and said to them, "If any one of you is without sin, let him be the first to throw a stone at her."*
>
> JOHN 8:3–7 NIV

There are times in our lives when most of us, if we would care to admit it, would not hesitate to throw a stone at someone else and put them down. By doing so, at least for that moment, we might feel that we have a bit more worth than them, but by doing so, we fall into the world's way of doing things. However, Paul shows us a much better way:

> *But eagerly desire the greater gifts.*
>
> *LOVE*
>
> *And now I will show you the most excellent way.*
>
> *If I speak in the tongues of men and of angels, but have not love, I am only a resounding gong or a clanging cymbal. If I have the gift of prophecy and can fathom all mysteries and all knowledge, and if I have a faith that can move mountains, but have not love, I am nothing. If I give all I possess to the poor and surrender my body to the flames, but have not love, I gain nothing.*

> *Love is patient, love is kind. It does not envy, it does not boast, it is not proud. It is not rude, it is not self-seeking, it is not easily angered, it keeps no record of wrongs. Love does not delight in evil but rejoices with the truth. It always protects, always trusts, always hopes, always perseveres.*
>
> *Love never fails. But where there are prophecies, they will cease; where there are tongues, they will be stilled; where there is knowledge, it will pass away.*
>
> 1 CORINTHIANS 12:31–13:8 NIV

Jesus came to set the captives free, and He has commanded us to do likewise.

> *He said to them, "Go into all the world and preach the gospel to all creation. Whoever believes and is baptized will be saved, but whoever does not believe will be condemned. And these signs will accompany those who believe: In my name they will drive out demons; they will speak in new tongues; they will pick up snakes with their hands; and when they drink deadly poison, it will not hurt them at all; they will place their hands on sick people, and they will get well."*
>
> MARK 16:15–18 NIV

## Chapter 12
# What about Deliverance Ministry?

'Deliverance' can be defined as: release, emancipation, escape, liberation, ransom, redemption, rescue and salvation.

Many people have strange ideas as to what deliverance ministry is. Some people have weird ideas that as soon as you start praying for people who are depressed etc., evil spirits start manifesting themselves, throwing stuff around the room trying to scare the life out of everyone, including Christians. Yes, we have seen some of this and have had to take authority over evil spirits but that is not the norm. From what we have observed, it is people who have consciously or inadvertently made a pact with the devil or opened doors to him, that struggle with demons.

There are various ways that doors could have been opened:

- Taking part in séances
- Reading books on witchcraft
- Watching the wrong kind of movies e.g. *Blair Witch Project*
- Playing with Ouija boards
- Having a palm reading
- Sending locks of hair for divination
- Consulting a psychic
- Making blood pacts
- Hypnosis
- Acupuncture
- Voodoo

- Involvement in martial arts or yoga
- Freemasons or other secret orders
- Drug abuse

These are but a few doorways to the occult. Anything that has a strong hold on us is a stronghold. The good news is, Jesus came to set us free from strongholds.

> *For though we live in the world, we do not wage war as the world does. The weapons we fight with are not the weapons of the world. On the contrary, they have divine power to demolish strongholds. We demolish arguments and every pretension that sets itself up against the knowledge of God, and we take captive every thought to make it obedient to Christ.*
>
> 2 CORINTHIANS 10:3–5 NIV

If they, their parents, grandparents, or great-grandparents have been involved in any of the above, these generational ties need to be broken. Individuals are not guilty for the sins of their parents, but they will have been influenced greatly by their family culture and heritage, which means that even though they may not have participated in any of these things, they have certainly been influenced, to one degree or another, by these demonic spirits. The Word of God shows us how to deal with generational sins.

> *But if they will confess their sins and the sins of their fathers—their treachery against me and their hostility toward me, which made me hostile toward them so that I sent them into the land of their enemies—then when their uncircumcised hearts are humbled and they pay for their sin, I will remember my covenant with Jacob and my covenant with Isaac and my covenant with Abraham, and I will remember the land.*
>
> LEVITICUS 26:40–42 NIV

> *Those of Israelite descent had separated themselves from all foreigners. They stood in their places and confessed their sins and the wickedness of their fathers.*
>
> NEHEMIAH 9:2 NIV

Many people are set free from these influences from the day they invite Christ into their lives, but others need further help in breaking these ties. This may be a concept that is completely new for some folks. If they are hesitant, suggest that they take some time to consider this and get back to you when they are ready. I have generally found that because of the freedom they have already received, they are prepared to step out in faith and trust the Lord for freedom in this regard. An excellent Christian book to read about being set free from ancestral sins is *Bloodline*, by Nalini Tranquim.

Key Scriptures I use regarding this are: Deuteronomy 18:9–14, Exodus 20:3–6, Proverbs 28:13 (NIV), Matthew 18:21–35, 1 John 1:9

To help make it easier for them to understand the importance of dealing with generational sins, I will talk about pruning unproductive branches and/or root pruning, both of which are important when dealing with unproductive fruit trees. However, we are now talking about spiritual pruning. Two Scriptures that I often refer to here are John 15:1–2 and Luke 3:9.

> *I am the true vine, and my Father is the gardener. He cuts off every branch in me that bears no fruit, while every branch that does bear fruit he prunes so that it will be even more fruitful.*
>
> JOHN 15:1–2 NIV

> *The ax is already at the root of the trees, and every tree that does not produce good fruit will be cut down and thrown into the fire.*
>
> LUKE 3:9 NIV

When they are ready, remind them of Ephesians 6:10–18 and particularly the Sword of the Spirit, which is the Word of God. After they have confessed the sins of their fathers, it is time to prune those unproductive branches and roots. Pray aloud and take authority over them using the Word of God and symbolically cut them, in Jesus' mighty Name.

As a visual illustration for the person I am working with, I often symbolically "pick up" those dead branches/roots and tell the person I am throwing them into the spiritual fire to be burned, never to regrow again.

Demons are like rats; they can only survive on rubbish. Jesus came to set the captives free. By getting rid of the rubbish in their lives, the demons have nothing to feed on. Knowing this in their heads does not bring freedom, it is only when they appropriate Jesus' work on the cross by faith, that freedom comes. Do not, at any time, 'entertain' demons by letting them speak because they will play games with you. They only speak lies and twist the truth; even the truth of God's Word!

> *And He cured many who were afflicted with various diseases; and He drove out many demons, but would not allow the demons to talk, because they knew Him [intuitively].*
>
> MARK 1:34 AMPLIFIED BIBLE

We are sons and daughters of the living God, and all the fullness of God indwells us (Colossians 2:9–10), so we have all the authority we need to command demons to remain silent.

Demons also know the Word of God. Satan used it to try and cause Jesus to stumble during the Wilderness Temptation, and he will use it to his advantage as soon as he becomes aware that you do not know the truth of God's Word and the authority that is rightfully yours.

> *Some Jews who went around driving out evil spirits tried to invoke the name of the Lord Jesus over those who were demon-possessed. They would say, "In the name of the Jesus whom Paul preaches, I command you to come out." Seven sons of Sceva, a Jewish chief priest, were doing this. One day the evil spirit answered them, "Jesus I know, and Paul I know about, but who are you?"*
>
> ACTS 19:13–15 NIV

We were once called in the middle of the night by frantic Christians who had been trying to minister to someone who was manifesting demons. We responded by telling them that another night was not going to make any difference, then we told them to command the demons to be silent and then to leave the person alone until a more appropriate day and time.

Even if you've never witnessed anyone manifesting demons before, when the time comes, and as long as you know the authority that is yours in Christ, you'll be able to command them to leave, in Jesus' Name.

There are many cultures and people around the world who are fully aware of the spiritual realm. Surprisingly, even as a child growing up in the UK, I knew there was more to life than what was seen with the physical eye. Church at that time didn't give me the answers I was looking for because, sadly, the Jesus I learned about at that time was only a great man who lived and walked this earth over 2,000 years ago but who had little or no relevance to my daily life.

My own search into the spiritual realm opened doors into the occult without me consciously being aware of it. Doors were opened to me by playing with Ouija boards, having my palm read, attending séances, reading books on the 'Third Eye', and practicing yoga, etc.

After I was born-again and met some Spirit-filled Christians, they showed me the way to freedom. I asked them to pray with me because I had tried doing it on my own, but I was not convinced that anything had happened. They asked me to write down on a piece of paper all the areas I had been involved in.

When it was time for me to pray, I could see a battle raging in full technicolour between the demons and the angels in the heavenly realms. I remember hearing my own voice sounding afar off crying out, "Jesus, help me!" As my Christian friends became aware of the battle that was taking place, they started doing spiritual warfare. An overwhelming sense of peace flooded my soul, and I was able to confess and renounce each one of those areas by name and I was set free. It seriously felt like a great weight had lifted off my shoulders!

A prisoner can't show a fellow prisoner the way to freedom, but because I was set free that day, I was determined to become better equipped so that I could show other people the way to freedom in Christ. It was remarkable! Just as a prisoner receives freedom when they are released from prison, I was truly liberated. It was not rocket science; it was so simple, and a great weight lifted off my shoulders. I skipped home rejoicing, and I could hardly wait to tell my husband what had happened. John 8:31–32 became a reality in my life.

At different stages while working through the Genogram, and especially if there has been any involvement in demonic activities, they will need to confess and renounce their involvement in them.

> *He who conceals his sins does not prosper,*
> *but whoever confesses and renounces them finds mercy.*
>
> PROVERBS 28:13 NIV

Confessing their sins means they are agreeing with God that what they have done is wrong, and renouncing their sins means they are making a proclamation in the heavenly realms that they will not be involved in them anymore. This is a vital step they will need to take to be set free. What we have noticed is, while they are confessing and renouncing their involvement in these activities, a kind of 'self-deliverance' takes place, which means it has not been necessary for us to engage in active spiritual warfare.

You cannot pray these prayers on their behalf, but as they pray, continue praying quietly and in agreement with them as they forgive those who have caused them pain, and as they close the door on all demonic activity. Keep your eyes open while all this is happening because you need to observe their body language to gauge if there is a spiritual blockage somewhere, or if they are receiving freedom in Christ.

If you are sensing a blockage, then sensitively share whatever that is with them. Take up the authority that is rightfully yours in Christ and pray audibly against those blockages. Their freedom in Christ is based solely on what Christ accomplished for them on the cross. Isaiah 61:1–3 is the Scripture that often comes to mind, so I stand on these promises for the person I am working with.

By the time they have finished forgiving all the wavy and zigzag underlined people, asked for forgiveness for the sins they have committed against them, and confessed and renounced any demonic involvement, many of the folks have shared how they have experienced a physical releasing. The most common phrase I hear is, "I feel lighter!" The weight of sin has been lifted and the result is felt in their physical bodies. It is a truly remarkable experience. I generally notice a complete difference in their countenance and their physical posture because many of them stand taller. There is generally a visible sign of joy in their hearts because they have been set free. I then ask them what they would like to do with the Genogram and most people respond by tearing it up and throwing it in the bin, others literally want to burn it. If that is their preference, find a safe place for them to do so.

Whatever stage you end at, always pray for a fresh filling of God's Spirit over the person before they leave and encourage them to continue being filled (Ephesians 5:18). Highlight the importance of regular Christian fellowship and a systematic reading of the

Word of God. Encourage them to report back to you every now and again with their progress, as this gives them a measure of accountability.

Most of them leave with a skip in their step and a new song in their heart. Just before they leave, I give them the sheets with the diagrams and all the Scriptures referred to during the session. We serve a miracle working God, and He chooses to use ordinary people, like us, to do extraordinary things in the power of the Holy Spirit.

May this book be used of the Lord to help you bring freedom, wholeness, and restoration, both to you and to those you minister to in Jesus' Name. Amen.

www.ingramcontent.com/pod-product-compliance
Lightning Source LLC
Chambersburg PA
CBHW061730070526
44583CB00024B/3085